About the Author

Kumkum Ahluwalia is a trained paediatrician and an accidental poet. She also likes to think of herself as a student of spirituality and believes in the power of meditation to heal, guide and nurture creativity. *Birdsong* is her debut project.

Birdsong

Kumkum Ahluwalia

Birdsong

Olympia Publishers
London

www.olympiapublishers.com
OLYMPIA PAPERBACK EDITION

Copyright © Kumkum Ahluwalia 2024

The right of Kumkum Ahluwalia to be identified as author of this work has been asserted in accordance with sections 77 and 78 of the Copyright, Designs and Patents Act 1988.

All Rights Reserved

No reproduction, copy or transmission of this publication may be made without written permission.
No paragraph of this publication may be reproduced, copied or transmitted save with the written permission of the publisher, or in accordance with the provisions of the Copyright Act 1956 (as amended).

Any person who commits any unauthorised act in relation to this publication may be liable to criminal prosecution and civil claims for damage.

A CIP catalogue record for this title is available from the British Library.

ISBN: 978-1-80439-670-4

This is a work of fiction.
Names, characters, places and incidents originate from the writer's imagination. Any resemblance to actual persons, living or dead, is purely coincidental.

First Published in 2024

Olympia Publishers
Tallis House
2 Tallis Street
London
EC4Y 0AB

Printed in Great Britain

Dedication

I dedicate this book to my spiritual teacher, Sant Rajinder Singh Ji Maharaj.

For Jumper

My furry friend left me
For years, he kept me
Though bereft, I'm not forlorn
For years of friendship are nothing to mourn.

The Call

Beyond the asphalt and clay
Wild ducks and egrets play
No longer can I stay.

A Tribute

One day, a few years ago
The agent said, "Come on, let's go!"
"Where now must we go?"
"To a magical place and don't be slow."

The hollowed grounds, the mud so brown
Did not put on much of a show
But as we drove through the barren land
The gut perceived what the mind did not know.

The welcoming arms of a land so new
Interlaced with a cup of Joe
Was everything the soul desired
I said, "No further need we go."

The mystery of the surrounding wildlife
Did cause my curiosity to grow
If they can survive, come rain or snow
We too can endure life's next blow.

So, it has been a magical time
To live amongst birds galore
And when the stars shine at night
There's a sense of peace not known before.

Irony of Love

As I walk through the woods
There's a whisper and a scream
As I traverse the muddy brooks
There's a knowing and a dream.

The beauty that was imparted
Has etched a memory so deep
That the image of the departed
Surfaces even in my sleep.

The beloved that is unseen
Soothes the calluses of my feet
Moonlight beckoning with its sheen
Prompts an urging to retreat.

The silence of the night
Made louder by the chirp
Of a cricket out of sight
Whose ache I don't disturb.

The journey continues in the haze
Of a vision in clear view
Walking alone in a daze
Careful not to step on you.

Sunbathing With the Geese

The sunbathers have come
The honking has begun
I stop what I'm doing and sprawl in the sun
In that moment, nature and I are one.

Wishing for Rain

I wish it would rain
Like that time in Spain
When we got wet and did not complain.

I wish it would rain
So, the mallards can dance
Prodding the heron and the crane.

I wish it would rain
So, the geese can clean
Their dusty feet in the billowing lane.

I wish it would rain
So, the starlings can alight
On the grass and circle the drain.

I wish it would rain
So, the robins would sing
A melody to tame any pain.

Birdsong

The day begins prematurely
It's unclear what's robbed sleep
Moving curtains reveals the thieves
Of a slumber that was just getting deep.

A few are gold and blue
With quills seemingly attached with glue
And others still with glowing bills
Wondrous shapes and magical trills.

Wonder what the day holds for them?
Will they dance in hay or frolic in sun?
But this is the moment that's true
The approaching day betrays no clue.

There's another dance less true
With jolting brew and broken shoe
Hurried steps and doors slammed shut
Conversations stopped and discourses cut.

The sun now golden, curtains closing
Trigger an unexpected unfolding
Is there another sort of day –
One meant to just be danced away?

The Silent Pond

There is a pond near my house
With beavers and ducks, even a mouse
When I get near, they disappear
Is it because they fear the kind
That inhabited earth without them in mind?

2020

Lives truncated; births celebrated
Paradigms created; traditions denounced
With local strife reflecting global plight
We are breathless resting in the longest night.

The sky's more blue
The smile more true
The act more considerate
The conversation more deliberate.

I'm aware of the birds and the geese
While waiting for dawn, I listen to the trees.

Where Did the Moon Go

Where did the moon go?
What did it know?
What did it say
About what I don't know?

Where did the moon go?
It was all aglow
One minute fast, next slow
One minute high, next low.

Where did the moon go?
With its sublime glow
Pristine like the snow
And eyes like a doe.

Where did the moon go?
I want so much to know
About the places I ought to go
And people I should know.

I look around but don't know
If I too must go
As fellow travellers have so
Surely the moon must know.

The Lake at Night

It comes alive at night
When the feathered ones alight
After a day of adventure
To plan a new venture.

I hurry past but find
A sudden need to rewind
I change my direction
And bestow deserved attention.

In V formation they land
The strongest helping the band
The show induces shame
Why can't we do the same?

In close proximity they move
In a quiet and familiar groove
I'm mesmerised by the lake
Beauty more than I can take.

The next day I return
Before the sun can burn
But I'm sad to find
Gone those I left behind.

The Lone Duck

It comes to me at night
When I consider what to write
That birds of different feathers can flock with ease
As I think of the lone duck in a gaggle of geese.

The Hill

The spectacle was hard to ignore
The hill held special allure
The circling went on for quite some time
Then all left leaving two behind.

The hill grew before my eyes
There were twigs and straw and things of surprise
The friendly neighbour was at the door
But I kept watching as before.

They seemed to have no need to eat
This matter really had me beat
No time to cook, food I did order
And rapidly consumed human fodder.

Then one sunny morning they were gone
No exaggeration, I was forlorn
I missed the sight and the sound
What did happen on that mound?

I watched the hill with bated breath
Nothing seemed to help the dread
But before my spirits felt too low
I saw them gliding, goslings in tow.

I'll Be Over There Watching the Ducks

Let's talk of good things yet to come
And imbibe a brew better than rum
But if you think life simply sucks
I'll be over there watching the ducks.

Let's talk about art and books and movies too
How they kept us from feeling blue
But if you play songs that sound like trucks
I'll be over there watching the ducks.

Let's talk about the value of every soul
With individual gifts and collective role
But if you measure their worth in bucks
I'll be over there watching the ducks.

An Ideal Mate

Geese mate for life
Mallards for a season.

The mallards are colourful
But I'm no fool.

The Dream Unfolds

The unfolding of the dream
Wasn't exactly as seen
But the beauty of the way
Did soften the dismay.

The flowing of the stream
More tumultuous than serene
But the vision of the water
The chaos could not alter.

The singing of the bird
Was no longer heard
But the dancing of the soul
Deprived hearing of its role.

The devastation and despair
Left much to repair
But the promise of the new
Inspired hope that only grew.

The moments filled with doubt
Allowed confidence to sprout
These were not moments lost
Epic growth at some cost.

First Dance

Let's dance together
Let's walk together
Hold my hands as you hold my gaze
Let's prance into better days.

The lands we travel
The mysteries we unravel
Might help those yet to come
And inspire songs not yet sung.